HISTORY MAKERS

HISTORY MAKERS
of the
SCIENTIFIC
REVOLUTION

NINA MORGAN

ILLUSTRATED BY
JESSICA CURTIS

Wayland

HISTORY MAKERS

Notes for teachers

History Makers uses a wide range of exciting contemporary sources – quotations, letters, paintings and artefacts – to build up detailed and informative portraits of people who made important contributions both to their own time and to the way we live now.

This book:

- features important figures from all areas of the Scientific Revolution – chemistry, physics, astronomy, natural sciences, philosophy and education.

- presents contemporary reactions to changes and innovations;

- focuses on the background to the Scientific Revolution and the changes it made to the lives and beliefs of people at all levels of society;

- emphasizes the importance of the era for modern life.

© First published in 1995 by
Wayland (Publishers) Ltd
61 Western Road, Hove,
East Sussex BN3 1JD,
England

© Copyright 1995 Wayland (Publishers) Ltd

Series editor: Katie Roden
Series designer: Tracy Gross
Book designer: Joyce Chester

British Library Cataloguing in Publication Data

Morgan, Nina
History Makers of the Scientific
Revolution.–(History Makers Series)
I. Title II. Curtis, Jessica III. Series
590.22

ISBN 0 7502 1549 6

Typeset by Dorchester Typesetting Group Ltd, England
Printed and bound in Italy by Rotolito

Picture acknowledgements:
E. T. Archive 11 (top), 12, 22, 32; Ann Ronan/Image Select 6, 7, 8, 9 (bottom), 10, 13, 14, 16, 17, 18 (top), 19, 20, 23, 24, 26 (both), 27, 28, 29, 30 (top), 31 (right), 33, 34, 39 (bottom), 40, 41, 42; Science Museum 9 (top), 11 (bottom), 18 (bottom), 25, 30 (bottom), 31 (left), 36 (top), 38, 43; Topham Picture Source 39 (top); Wayland Picture Library 20, 21, 35, 36 (bottom), 37 (both).

C o n t e n t s

Words in **bold** in the text are explained in the glossary on page 44.

Nicolaus Copernicus

1473 - 1543

'This fool wishes to reverse the entire science of **astronomy***!'*

This is what Martin Luther, the founder of the **Lutheran Church**, had to say when he learned of the work of Nicolaus Copernicus.

Like many people living in the sixteenth century, Luther believed that the Earth was the centre of the universe, and that the Sun and the planets moved around it. This seemed reasonable to most people, because when they looked at the sky at night, all the stars and planets did appear to move past the Earth. But, after studying all the evidence, Copernicus came up with a new and shocking idea. He said that the Earth and all the planets travelled around the Sun.

A seventeenth-century drawing of the Copernican solar system, showing the planets orbiting the Sun.

Nicolaus Copernicus was born in Torun, Poland, in 1473. He studied first at Krakow University in Poland, and later at several universities in Italy. Although he studied many different subjects, his greatest interest was in astronomy. While still a student, Copernicus began to observe the stars and planets. He soon realized that what he saw could only be understood if the Earth and the planets travelled around the Sun. In 1514, Copernicus wrote a short summary of his ideas for his friends to study.

Copernicus did not publish or discuss his ideas in public, because he was afraid that they would shock too many people. He was especially worried about upsetting the Catholic Church, which believed that the Earth and all the people on it were the perfect creations of God. Copernicus wrote:

> *'... I was almost impelled to put the finished work wholly aside, through the scorn I had reason to anticipate on account of the newness and apparent contrariness to reason of my theory.'*

However, towards the end of his life, Copernicus was persuaded to publish his ideas in a book called *De Revolutionibus Orbium Coelestium (On the Revolutions of the Heavenly Spheres)*. Although he never lived to see it, the work of Copernicus opened the way for astronomy to become a modern science.

Copernicus finally allowed his ideas to be published in 1543, the year he died. They were discussed in his book *De Revolutionibus Orbium Coelestium*.

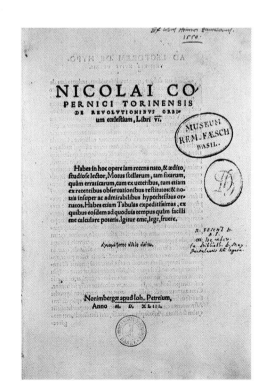

OTHERS TO STUDY

Tycho Brahe (1546–1601) – a Danish astronomer and mathematician. Although he worked before the telescope had been invented, he made many important observations of the stars and planets.

Johanes Kepler (1571–1630) – a German astronomer who showed that the orbits of the planets were not circular.

Galileo Galilei (1564–1642) – see pages 8–11.

DATE CHART

1473
19 February: Copernicus is born in Torun, Poland.

1496–1503
Studies in Italy.

1503
Returns to Poland.

1514
Writes about his theory that the planets travel round the Sun rather than the Earth, in a paper for his friends only.

1543
Publishes his ideas in his book, *De Revolutionibus Orbium Coelestium*.
24 May: Dies just after his book is published.

Galileo Galilei

1564 - 1642

'I do not hold, and have not held, this opinion of Copernicus since the command was intimated to me that I must abandon it.'

Although Galileo Galilei spoke these words in 1633, he certainly did not believe them. Using telescopes that he built himself, Galileo made observations which convinced him that the astronomer Copernicus was right when he wrote in 1543 that all the planets, including the Earth, travelled around the Sun.

Galileo, who is known only by his first name, was born in Pisa, Italy, in 1564, and grew up in Florence. In 1581, when he was 17, he went to the University of Pisa to study medicine. But he soon realized that he was much more interested in mathematics and physics.

Galileo was one of the first scientists to test his theories by carrying out experiments. This drawing shows his experiment to find the breaking point of a board.

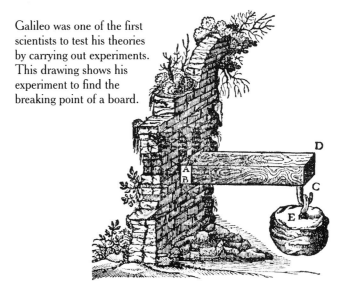

Galileo began his scientific career by carrying out research in physics. In his work, he used mathematical calculations to describe what he saw, and showed how mathematics could be a useful tool for physicists. He was also one of the first scientists to test his theories by setting up experiments which anyone could repeat.

In 1609, when he first heard of the invention of the telescope, Galileo began to study the sky. He soon built his own improved versions of the telescope, and began looking at the Moon, stars and planets.

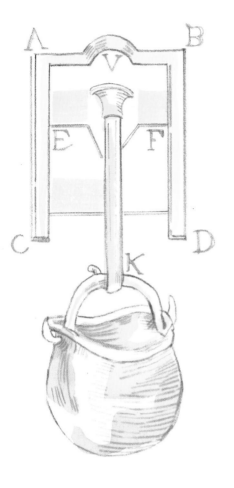

Two of the many telescopes that Galileo used to study the Moon, stars and planets.

Through his telescopes, Galileo was the first person to see that the Moon was not smooth, as most people believed, but rough and covered with mountains and valleys. He also discovered many new stars, and noticed that the planet Jupiter was circled by four moons of its own.

OTHERS TO STUDY

William Gilbert (1544–1603) – a British physicist and doctor who, like Galileo, used scientific methods of observation and experimentation in his studies. His main work was on magnets and magnetism.

Francis Bacon (1561–1626) – a British scientist who, like Galileo, believed in using first-hand observations to come up with theories. He also worked to find the relationships between all branches of science.

Nicolaus Copernicus (1473–1543) – see pages 6–7.

These new sights convinced him that Copernicus's ideas were right. In 1610, Galileo published his own ideas in Latin in a book called *Sidereus Nuncius (The Starry Messenger)*. The book was very popular, and converted many people to the Copernican view. However, it also angered the Catholic Church, which taught that God had created the Earth as the centre of the universe.

In 1616, the Catholic authorities in Rome **condemned** the Copernican system and banned Galileo from teaching or writing about it. But Galileo did not give up.

On the title page of his book *Dialogue on the Two Chief World Systems*, published in 1632, Galileo demonstrated his respect for the astronomer Copernicus by showing him talking to the famous ancient Greek scientists Aristotle and Ptolemy.

A few years later, he persuaded the Pope, the head of the Catholic Church, to allow him to write a 'balanced' account of the arguments. The result was his book *Dialogue on the Two Chief World Systems*, published in 1632. The book was written in Italian and quickly sold out. But it was not a very fair account. In the book, Galileo named the character who supported the Church 'Simplico' (simple), and made him seem stupid.

The Pope was furious. Galileo was tried by the Church court and was forced to make a public statement saying that he did not believe in the Copernican view. He was also sentenced to **house arrest** for the rest of his life, and was banned from publishing any more books.

This punishment did not stop Galileo from working on his ideas of motion, in which he tried to describe the movement of things such as falling objects. He wrote about this work in Italian, and a friend smuggled the manuscript to the Netherlands. There it was published in 1638 under the title *Discourses and Mathematical Demonstrations concerning Two New Sciences*. The next year, Galileo became ill. He died in Arcetri, near Florence, Italy, in 1642.

In 1633, Galileo, shown here wearing black and sitting on a red chair, was tried by the Church court. As a result of the trial, Galileo was forced to make a statement saying that he did not believe in the Copernican theory.

Galileo's ideas have continued to influence scientists ever since. One of his many modern admirers was the twentieth-century physicist Albert Einstein. He wrote:

'All knowledge of reality starts from experience and ends in it ... Because Galileo saw this, and particularly because he drummed it into the scientific world, he is the father of modern physics – indeed of modern science altogether.'

The Roman Catholic Church was slower to see the value of Galileo's achievements. It did not forgive him officially until 1979.

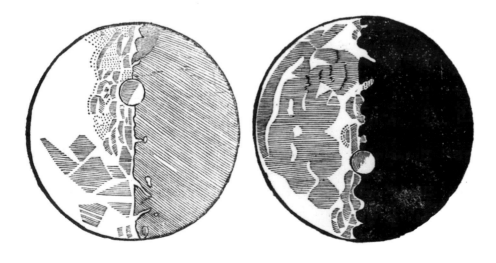

These drawings by Galileo show the rough surface of the Moon. Galileo was the first person to observe that the surface of the Moon was rough, rather than smooth as most people thought.

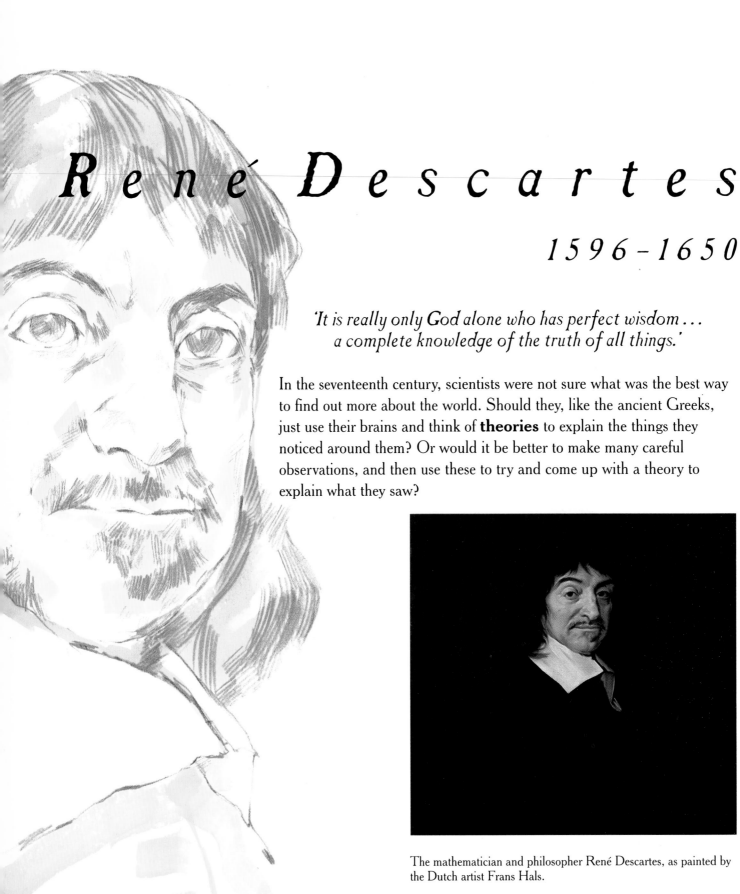

René Descartes

1596–1650

*'It is really only God alone who has perfect wisdom…
a complete knowledge of the truth of all things.'*

In the seventeenth century, scientists were not sure what was the best way to find out more about the world. Should they, like the ancient Greeks, just use their brains and think of **theories** to explain the things they noticed around them? Or would it be better to make many careful observations, and then use these to try and come up with a theory to explain what they saw?

The mathematician and philosopher René Descartes, as painted by the Dutch artist Frans Hals.

René Descartes believed that the answer to this problem was to do a little bit of both. He explained this in 1637, in his book *Discours de la Méthode (Discourse on Method)*, by saying:

*'... provided only that one **abstains** from accepting any for true which is not true, and that one always keeps the right order for one thing, to be **deduced** from that which precedes it, there can be nothing so distant that one does not reach it eventually, or so hidden that one cannot discover it.'*

In other words, if you start from a known fact, and use this as the basis for making more observations, there is nothing that you will not be able to understand.

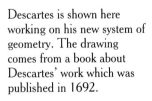

Descartes is shown here working on his new system of geometry. The drawing comes from a book about Descartes' work which was published in 1692.

René Descartes was born in Touraine, France, in 1596. He earned a degree in Law from the University of Poitiers in France in 1616, and then travelled throughout Europe as a soldier in the Dutch and Bavarian armies.

He soon became interested in working on problems in mathematics and **mechanics**. His goal was to set up a single, clear way to explain nature. In 1629 Descartes moved to Amsterdam in Holland, where he felt he would have more freedom to think about his new **philosophy**.

OTHERS TO STUDY

**Pierre de Fermat
(1601 – 65)**
– a French mathematician who, like Descartes, worked to develop analytical geometry.

**Apollonius of Perga
(third century BC)**
– an ancient Greek goemeter whose work inspired Descartes and other mathematicians.

13

Descartes started by doubting everything. One key question which he asked himself was 'How do I know that I exist?' His answer, published in *Discourse on Method*, was:

'Cogito ergo sum.'
('I think, therefore I am.')

This way of questioning and looking for proof before accepting any ideas influenced the way in which many scientists worked. It also led Descartes to use mathematics to try to explain how the universe worked.

In this toy, known as a Descartes' diver, tiny hollow figures floated in water inside a glass cylinder. When the stretchy film covering the surface was pressed, the water pressure inside the cylinder increased. This caused the water to flow into the diver through a small hole in its foot. The weight of the water made the diver sink to the bottom. When the pressure was released, the water flowed out of the diver and rose again.

DATE CHART

1596
31 March: René Descartes is born in Touraine, France.

1616
Receives a Law degree from the University of Poitiers.

1628
Begins to work on a new philosophical system about science.

1629
Moves to the Netherlands.

1637
Discourse on Method is published.

1649
Moves to Sweden, but dies after a few months.

To help himself in this study, Descartes invented analytical geometry – a new, mathematical way of looking at shapes and the relationships between objects. This new form of mathematics made it possible to carry out more complicated calculations than ever before.

He also thought up a system to describe the positions of objects, by measuring their distances from lines drawn at 90° from each other. This system was called Cartesian coordinates, after Descartes, and it is still used on many maps and to create accurate technical drawings of buildings or machines.

Descartes' work in mathematics and philosophy led him to come up with the idea that the movements of the universe are controlled by basic laws which were set out by God at the beginning of time. Descartes believed that the universe and everything in it ticked along according to set rules which could be worked out using mathematics. This idea of a 'clockwork' universe, a machine which could be understood as easily as the workings of a clock, influenced the work of many scientists.

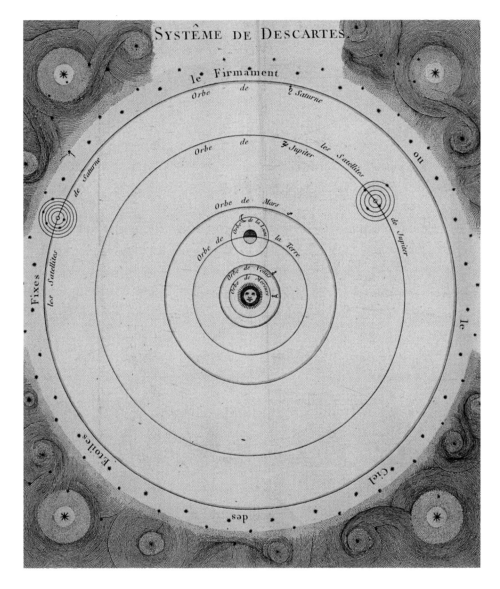

Like Copernicus, Descartes believed that the planets travelled around the Sun, as shown here in a print of Descartes' system, published in Paris, France in 1761.

Descartes' ideas also attracted the attention of Queen Christina of Sweden, a woman who had a strong interest in science. In 1649 she persuaded Descartes to accept her help and to move to Stockholm. Sadly, within a few months of arriving, Descartes caught an illness and died. But his ideas, and the mathematical methods he invented, lived on, and influenced the thoughts of many scientists who came after him.

Robert Boyle

1627 - 91

'The surest way is to learne by particular experiments what ... parts particular bodies do consist of ...'

In these words from his book *The Sceptical Chymist* (Chemist), published in 1661, the physicist and chemist Robert Boyle wrote about the need to conduct careful experiments in order to understand the chemistry of the world. Although this idea seems obvious to us today, in Boyle's time it caused much discussion. Then, many chemists still accepted the ideas presented in a 'science' known as alchemy.

Alchemists believed that the universe could be explained in terms of the four 'elements': earth, air, fire and water. To prove this, they conducted strange ceremonies instead of scientific experiments.

This picture, published in 1508, shows an alchemist at work.

16

Because of the way alchemists worked, many **natural scientists** and physicists – or 'natural philosophers' and 'mechanical philosophers' as they were known in the seventeenth century – believed that chemistry was not a true science. Boyle wanted to change this attitude. He tried through his work and writings to:

'... begat a good understanding betwixt the chymists and the mechanical philosophers.'

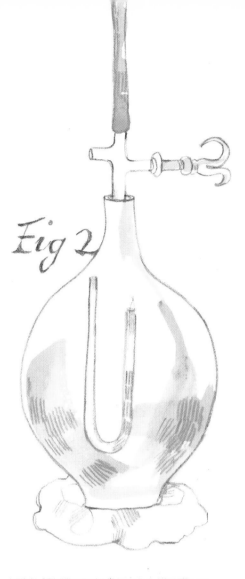

A portrait of Robert Boyle, published in 1740. The picture also shows some of the scientific instruments and books that Boyle used in his work.

Robert Boyle was born into a wealthy family in Lismore, County Cork, Ireland, in 1627. He received a good education and read many books about science, philosophy and religion. He also travelled in Europe and learned several languages.

In 1654, when he was 27 years old, he went to live in Oxford, England. Boyle soon made friends with many of the scientists studying at the university there. One of these was Robert Hooke, who became his assistant.

OTHERS TO STUDY

John Wallis (1616–1703) – a British scholar and mathematician who worked with Boyle to found the Royal Society.

Otto von Guericke (1602–86) – a German scientist who invented the improved vacuum pump, which Boyle used in his experiments. He also made the first electric machine and carried out experiments to demonstrate the elasticity of air.

Jan Baptiste van Helmont (1579–1644) – a Belgian doctor and chemist whose work inspired Boyle. He invented the word 'gas'.

A Table of the Rarefaction of the Air.

A	B	C	D	E
1	00 9/16		29 3/4	29 3/4
1½	10 1/16		19 1/2	19 7/16
2	15 5/16		14 3/8	14 7/8
3	20 1/4		9 5/16	9 11/16
4	22 3/8		7 3/16	7 7/16
5	24 3/8		5 3/16	5 12/16
6	24 7/8	Subtracted from 29 9/16 leaves	4 7/8	4 13/16
7	25 3/8		4 3/16	4 4/16
8	26 1/16		3 5/16	3 11/16
9	26 3/8		3 3/16	3 5/16
10	26 9/16		3 0	2 25/46
12	27 1/16		2 8/16	2 13/16
14	27 1/4		2 5/16	2 1/8
16	27 5/16		2 2/16	1 11/64
18	27 3/8		1 8/16	1 47/72
20	28 1/16		1 6/16	1 9/80
24	28 1/16		1 4/16	1 11/32
28	28 3/8		1 3/16	1 1/16
32	28 4/16		1 2/8	0 119/128

A. The number of equal spaces at the top of the Tube, that contained the same parcel of Air.
B. The height of the Mercurial Cylinder, that together with the Spring of the included Air counterbalanced the pressure of the Atmosphere.
C. The pressure of the Atmosphere.
D. The Complement of B to C, exhibiting the pressure sustained by the included Air.
E. What that pressure should be according to the Hypothesis.

This table, which Boyle published in 1682 in his book *Experiments Physico-Mechanicall*, helps to prove Boyle's Law. It lists the results of an experiment that Boyle carried out to show that at high pressures air will take up less space than the same amount of air at a lower pressure.

With Hooke's help, Boyle carried out experiments on gases using an air pump. In 1662 this work lead to the discovery of the 'ideal gas law', often known as Boyle's Law. This law states that:

'The volume of a given mass of gas at a constant temperature is inversely proportional to its pressure.'

This means that if the temperature remains the same, a gas at high **pressure** will take up less space than the same amount of the gas at a lower pressure. It also proved that gases are made up of small particles, or **atoms**, and that under high pressure the atoms which make up the gas are pushed together more closely than under low pressure. Boyle first wrote about this law in 1662 in his book called *Experiments Physico-Mechanicall*.

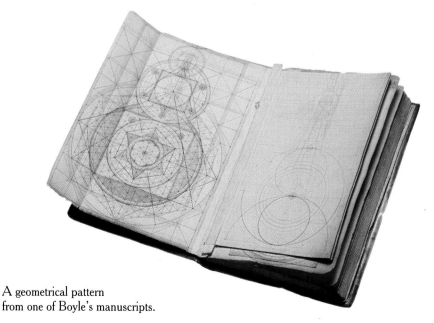

A geometrical pattern from one of Boyle's manuscripts.

Boyle also worked to understand what **chemical elements** were. In *The Sceptical Chymist*, Boyle wrote about elements as:

'... simple, or perfectly unmingled bodies; which not being made of any other bodies, or of one another, are the ingredients of which all those called perfectly mixt bodies are immediately compounded, and into which they are ultimately resolved.'

In other words, Boyle defined elements as substances which cannot be split up into separate parts. This is very close to the definition that chemists use today.

Boyle studied and wrote about many other subjects, including crystals and the origin of colours. In addition, he became very interested in medicine, and wrote several books on medical subjects.

In 1662, Boyle joined other Oxford scientists to found the Royal Society, a famous institution devoted to the study of science. Boyle gave many public lectures at the Royal Society because he believed it was important that science should be open to everyone, including women.

Throughout his life, Boyle refused to accept any honours or titles for his work. When he died in London in 1691, he left behind many important ideas about the role of atoms and the importance of doing carefully planned experiments. These influenced many later scientists. Boyle's work forms the basis of many modern scientific theories.

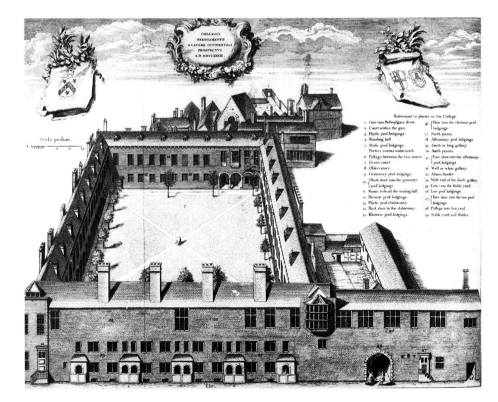

Gresham College in London. This was the first home of the Royal Society, an institution devoted to the promotion of science.

Women in the Scientific Revolution

'All things of an abstracted Nature are Incomprehensible to them. They cannot employ their Imagination in disentangling compound and perplex'd Questions.'

This is what Nicolas Malebrouche, a French philosopher, wrote in 1700 about the way women think. His view was quite a common one. During the seventeenth century, many men did not believe that women were able to understand 'complicated' ideas. As a result, girls were not usually given as good an education as boys, or taught 'difficult' subjects such as Latin or Greek.

Bathsua Maken was a well-educated woman who set up a school for girls in 1763. Her aim was to help girls to make the most of their talents. At her school, science formed an important part of the studies.

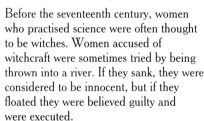

To many women, this waste of their brain power and talents seemed very silly, as explained by Bathsua Maken:

'Had God intended women only as a finer sort of cattle, he would not have made them reasonable.'

Maken was a well-educated woman who became tutor to the children of King Charles I of Britain in 1641. Among the many subjects she taught were science and mathematics. In 1763 she set up a school for girls. Her aim was to help girls make the most of their talents. At her school, science formed an important part of their studies.

Before the seventeenth century, women who practised science were often thought to be witches. Women accused of witchcraft were sometimes tried by being thrown into a river. If they sank, they were considered to be innocent, but if they floated they were believed guilty and were executed.

In medieval times and beyond, women who practised science ran the risk of being thought witches and put to death. By the seventeenth century, however, science was becoming a very respectable and fashionable subject to study. Intelligent women began to see science as an ideal way to make use of their talents. All they needed to make important contributions to science was a good brain, lots of imagination, a willingness to concentrate and work, and lots of free time. These were things which many well-to-do women had in plenty.

However, in spite of all the research they carried out, women's names did not often appear in scientific papers during the seventeenth and eighteenth centuries. This was because it was not thought proper that women should publish their work under their own names.

Nevertheless, there were many women who made important contributions to science. Sometimes this came about because they used their position in society to support male scientists. For example, Queen Christina of Sweden offered help to the French scientist René Descartes.

Queen Christina of Sweden used her wealth and position to help the French scientist René Descartes.

Sometimes it was the women themselves who made the scientific breakthroughs. In France, the Marquise du Châtelet (1706–49) and Sophie Germain (1776–1831) made important contributions to the study of mathematics. In Italy, Maria Agnesi (1718–99) helped to develop **calculus**. In Britain, the astronomer Caroline Herschel discovered three new clouds of stars in 1783. However, like many women scientists of the time, she had to keep quiet about her achievements, and all the credit for her work went to her brother William.

Caroline Herschel helped her brother, the astronomer William Herschel, to record the data which led to many of his discoveries, including the discovery of the planet Uranus. She also made many discoveries of her own, but the credit for these went to her brother.

Other women were more open about their achievements and were supported by their husbands and brothers, even though they were made fun of in public. Margaret Cavendish, the Duchess of Newcastle – known to some as 'Mad Madge of Newcastle' – attended scientific meetings and developed theories about the nature of the universe. She also encouraged other women to follow their interests in science. By the time she died in 1673, she had published several books about science and had received tributes from many educated men.

Other women, such as Elizabeth Carter (1717–1806) Margaret Bryan, who lived during the second half of the eighteenth century, and Aphra Behn (1640–89), wrote and translated explanations of scientific theories so that other women and men could understand them.

During the eighteenth century, more people began to realize that women were making valuable contributions to science. Many books, such as *The Ladies' Diary*, a yearly book packed with science and mathematics, were published especially for women interested in science. These helped to bring much new talent into the subject.

Although women often had to work behind the scenes, historians and scientists now realize what important contributions women made to the Scientific Revolution.

OTHERS TO STUDY

Sofie Brahe
– a sister of the astronomer Tycho Brahe, whom she helped to predict a lunar eclipse in 1573.

Electress Sophia of Hanover (1630–1714)
– a German princess who gave support to the German scientist Gottfried van Leibniz.

Lady Anne Conway (1631–79)
– a British scientist, whose theories were credited to the man who published them.

Marie-Anne Lavoisier (1758–1836)
– see page 40.

Lady Mary Wortley Montagu (1689–1762)
– introduced vaccination against the disease smallpox in Britain.

Anthony van Leeuwenhoek

1632 – 1723

'They stop, stand still as 'twere on a point and then turn themselves round with that swiftness as we see a top turn round, the **circumference** *they make being no bigger than that of a fine grain of sand.'*

This is how Anthony van Leeuwenhoek described his discovery of 'living animalcules' – tiny animals, or micro-organisms – in a drop of water, in a letter written in about 1674. His announcement astonished scientists throughout Europe. Leeuwenhoek saw the 'animalcules' using a microscope he made himself.

This portrait of Anthony van Leeuwenhoek describes him as a member of the Royal Society of London.

Anthony van Leeuwenhoek was born in Delft in the Netherlands, in 1632. After he left school he went to work in a fabric shop in Amsterdam. Soon he returned to Delft to open his own fabric business. He married and took up life as a respectable citizen – but one with a very unusual hobby: Leeuwenhoek liked to spend his spare time making microscopes.

Leeuwenhoek's microscopes were very different to those we use today. His microscopes were made of just one small **lens**, which was ground precisely by hand to form a glass bead. This tiny lens was set in a hole drilled into a brass plate.

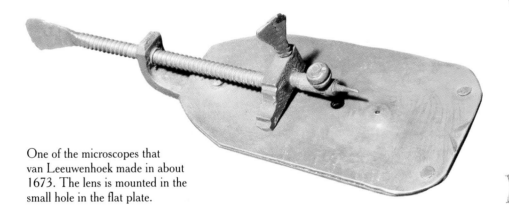

One of the microscopes that van Leeuwenhoek made in about 1673. The lens is mounted in the small hole in the flat plate.

The specimens Leeuwenhoek observed through his microscopes were mounted on a silver needle on one side of the lens. To use a microscope, he held it up to the light and looked at the specimen through the lens. The microscope was **focused** by moving the specimen nearer or farther from the lens, using an arrangement of moving pins.

Using the microscopes was very difficult and very tiring. But Leeuwenhoek became fascinated by the tiny objects he was able to see.

He used his microscopes to examine many common things, such as drops of water, mould and the mouths of bees. He even examined the scrapings from his own teeth. In 1683 he wrote a letter describing what he saw:

'…a little white matter, which is a thick as if 'twere batter… I almost always saw, with great wonder, that in the said matter there were many very little living animalcules, very prettily a-moving.'

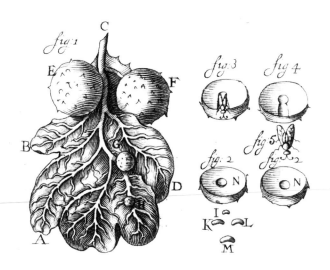

Van Leeuwenhoek made many detailed drawings of the objects he studied using his microscopes. In this drawing, he shows how small wasps develop on oak leaves, in growths known as galls.

Leeuwenhoek also used his microscopes to examine and describe, for the first time, sperm **cells** and red blood cells which he believed to carry food throughout the body. Sperm cells were later shown to be the cells that **fertilize** eggs when animals and humans **reproduce**.

Leeuwenhoek was curious to find out about all sorts of things. He was just as interested to use his microscopes to study the eyes of insects and the life cycles of fleas, aphids, ants and other insects as he was to examine other organisms.

Although Leeuwenhoek did not have a scientific education, and could not speak or write in English, in 1680 he was elected a member of the Royal Society of London, the most famous scientific society of the day. This honour brought him great fame. Many important people came to visit him and look through his microscopes.

DATE CHART

1632
24 October: Leeuwenhoek is born in Delft, the Netherlands.

1648
Is apprenticed to a draper in Amsterdam.

1654
Returns to Delft, marries and opens his own fabric business.

1660
Becomes a civil servant.

1671
Builds his first microscope.

1673
Leeuwenhoek's talent in building and using microscopes is brought to the attention of the Royal Society in London. Begins writing letters to the Royal Society.

1680
Elected as a member of the Royal Society.

1716
Awarded an honorary degree by the University of Louvain.

1723
Dies at the age of 91.

Van Leeuwenhoek wrote many letters in Dutch describing what he saw under his microscopes. This is the title page from a collection of his letters, published in 1685.

26

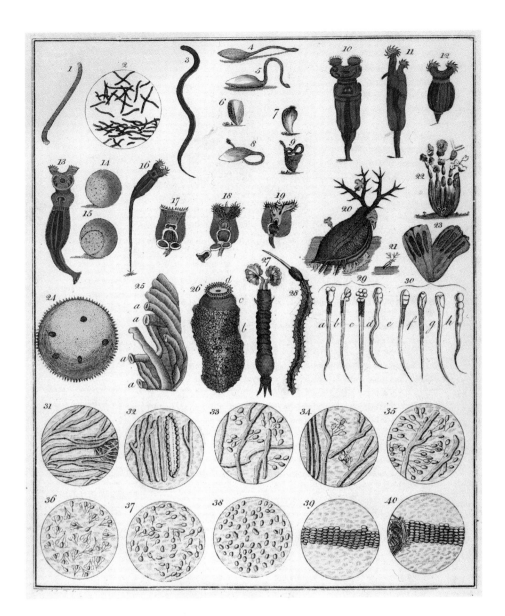

Drawings of some of the 'living animalcules' which van Leeuwenhoek saw using his microscopes. The drawings labelled 4-9 are of sperm cells.

But all this attention did not stop his work. Leeuwenhoek continued to observe and write letters in Dutch to the Royal Society until he died. Over 50 years, Leeuwenhoek wrote more than 370 letters describing his observations. Many of these were translated into English and published by the Society.

Leeuwenhoek also made over 400 microscopes. The most powerful ones could **magnify** objects 275 times. When he died at the age of 91, he left more than 200 microscopes and many lenses.

Leeuwenhoek's work opened up a new, invisible world to scientists throughout Europe. He helped to establish the microscope as a useful tool to gather facts and reveal exciting new views of nature.

OTHERS TO STUDY

Marcello Malpighi (1628–94) – an Italian microscopist who studied animals and discovered the small blood vessels known as capillaries.

Nehemiah Grew (1641–1712) – a British doctor and plant anatomist who used microscopes to study the structure of plants.

Jan Swammerdam (1637–80) – a Dutch microscopist who studied insects.

Robert Hooke

1635-1703

'The truth is, the Science of Nature has been already too long made only a work of the Brain and the Fancy: it is now high time that it should return to the plainness and soundness of Observations on material and obvious things.'

The British scientist Robert Hooke wrote these words in the preface to his book *Micrographia*, which was published in 1665. Hooke believed that observations were the key to understanding the world around him. But, unlike many scientists of the time, he also thought that observations and experiments should be carried out in an organized way in order to prove or disprove a theory.

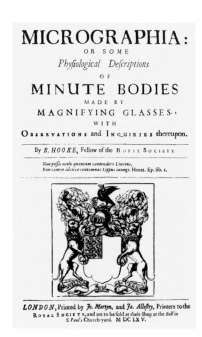

The title page from Robert Hooke's book *Micrographia*, which was published in 1665. The book included many detailed drawings of the objects that Hooke studied under his microscope.

28

Hooke published theories about the behaviour of light and colours and the motion of planets, and discussed his ideas with other important scientists. He also discovered the law of **elasticity**, or Hooke's Law. He summarized this law using the Latin words:

'Ut tensio, sic vis.'
('As is the tension, thus is the force.')

In other words, the amount by which something will stretch is related to the amount of force applied to it.

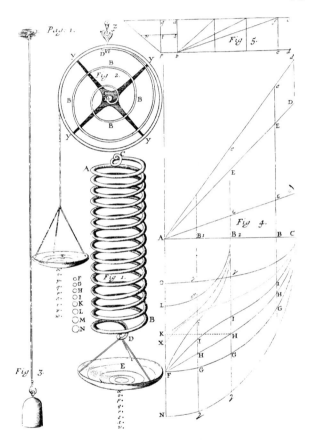

A drawing showing the coiled spring and weights which Hooke used to demonstrate Hooke's Law. By using heavier weights, Hooke could apply more force to the spring. By carrying out experiments, Hooke was able to show that the amount the spring stretched was related to the amount of force applied to it.

Robert Hooke was born in 1635 on the Isle of Wight, England. After studying at Westminster School in London, he entered Oxford University in 1653. While at Oxford he became an assistant to the chemist and physicist Robert Boyle. He helped Boyle to do the work that led to the discovery of Boyle's Law of the behaviour of gases.

In 1662, with a group of Oxford friends, Hooke helped to found the Royal Society of London, an organization set up to support science. He soon became Curator of Experiments at the Society. This job meant that Hooke had to think up many different interesting experiments and scientific demonstrations to present at the weekly Society meetings.

OTHERS TO STUDY

Robert Boyle (1627–91)
– see pages 16–19.

Christian Huygens (1596–1687)
– a Dutch physicist and astronomer who invented some of the instruments that Hooke used in his work.

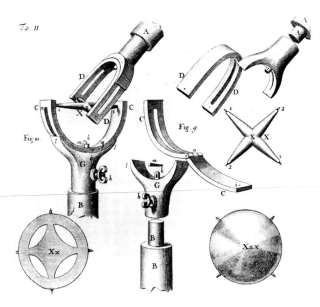

A drawing made by Hooke in 1676 to show the workings of the universal joint which he invented.

In order to do this, Hooke designed many new scientific instruments. His inventions included the spring control of the balance wheel in watches, a wheel **barometer** and the **universal joint**. He also built the first reflecting telescope, and invented the compound microscope. In this type of microscope, two lenses are placed either end of a tube to produce a better view.

One of Hooke's compound microscopes. Hooke invented this new type of microscope, which consists of two lenses placed at either end of a tube. The observer looked through an eyepiece at the top of the tube, and the specimen was placed on the plate near the base of the stand. Similar types of microscopes are still used today.

Hooke was interested in many different branches of science. He looked into problems in astronomy, physics and chemistry, and became fascinated by the miniature world he saw under his microscopes.

Hooke published his observations in 1665 in a book called *Micrographia* (Tiny Drawings). For this book, he made many beautiful and precise drawings which showed the things he had studied under the microscope. These included wonders such as the eye of a fly, the shape of a bee's stinger, the body of a flea and the structure of feathers. In addition, he described the cells in plants, and suggested that their purpose might be to carry fluids through the plant.

(left) A detailed drawing of a flea, as observed by Hooke using one of his microscopes. The drawing is from Hooke's book *Micrographia*, which was published in 1665.

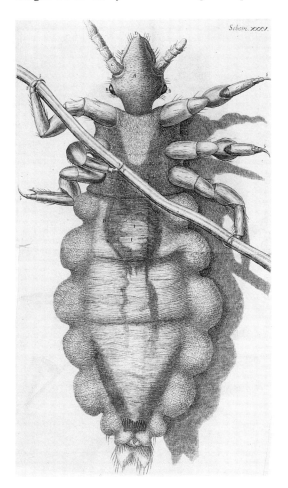

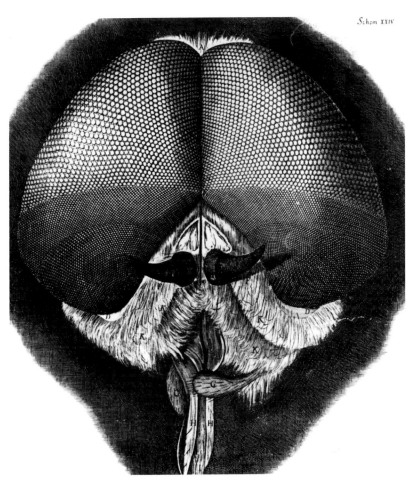

In *Micrographia*, Hooke also presented his view that **fossils** were the remains of living creatures. This idea was shocking to many people at that time, who believed that fossils were either placed on Earth by God or, like crystals, were formed by natural means.

By the time Hooke died in London in 1703, he had invented many new scientific instruments and made many important discoveries. He had also helped to build the Royal Society into the important body of scientists which it still is today.

(right) The compound eye of a fly seen under Hooke's microscope and published in his book *Micrographia*.

31

E d m u n d   H a l l e y

1656 - 1742

'...at the age of nineteen, he solved this useful problem in astronomie, never donne before... for which his name will be ever famous.'

This is how a seventeenth-century writer described Edmund Halley.

Halley was born in 1656, the son of a wealthy London soap manufacturer. When he went to study at Oxford University in 1673, his great interest was astronomy, the study of the stars and planets.

Halley published a book about astronomy while he was still a student at Oxford. The Astronomer Royal John Flamsteed, the chief astronomer in Britain, was just one of the many people who were impressed. He encouraged Halley to do more work in studying the stars and planets.

The astronomer Edmund Halley as an old man.

One of Halley's maps of the location of the stars in the southern hemisphere. The drawings of animals represent the different constellations, or groups, of stars.

OTHERS TO STUDY

Isaac Newton (1642–1727) – a British physicist and mathematician whom Halley greatly respected. Halley paid to have Newton's book *Principia Mathematica* published.

John Flamsteed (1646–1719) – the first Astronomer Royal and the author of several important star catalogues.

Christopher Wren (1632–1723) – a British architect and mathematician who, like Halley, worked to explain the orbits of the planets.

DATE CHART

1656
8 November: Edmund Halley is born.

1673
Goes to Oxford University.

1676
Travels to St Helena and charts the stars in the southern hemisphere.

1679
Publishes *Catalogus Stellarum Australium*.

1687
Pays to have Newton's book *Principia Mathematica* published.

1705
Publishes his work on comets and predicts the return of Halley's comet in 1758.

1720
Becomes Astronomer Royal.

1742
14 January: Dies.

1758
Halley's comet is seen, as he predicted.

Halley took his advice. At the age of 20 he published his book *Catalogus Stellarum Australium (Catalogue of the Southern Stars)*, which was based on observations he carried out on the Island of St Helena, off the coast of Africa.

The book made Halley famous. He was invited to join the Royal Society, an organization which promoted scientific research, where he met many famous scientists, including the physicist and mathematician Isaac Newton. Halley greatly encouraged Newton, and paid to have Newton's book *Principia Mathematica* published.

Newton was very grateful for this help and encouragement. In the preface to *Principia Mathematica* he wrote:

'In the publication of this *Work*, the most acute and universally learned *Mr Edmund Halley* not only assisted me with his pains in correcting the press and taking care of the *Schemes*, but it was to his **solicitations** that its becoming *publick* is owing.'

Meanwhile, Halley continued his own work in astronomy. After making a study of **comets**, Halley predicted that a particular comet which appeared in 1682 would reappear in 1758. Although Halley did not live to see it, he was right!

Halley's comet has been seen every 76 years since. Its latest appearance was in 1986. This time, astronomers were able to study it with the help of modern spacecraft.

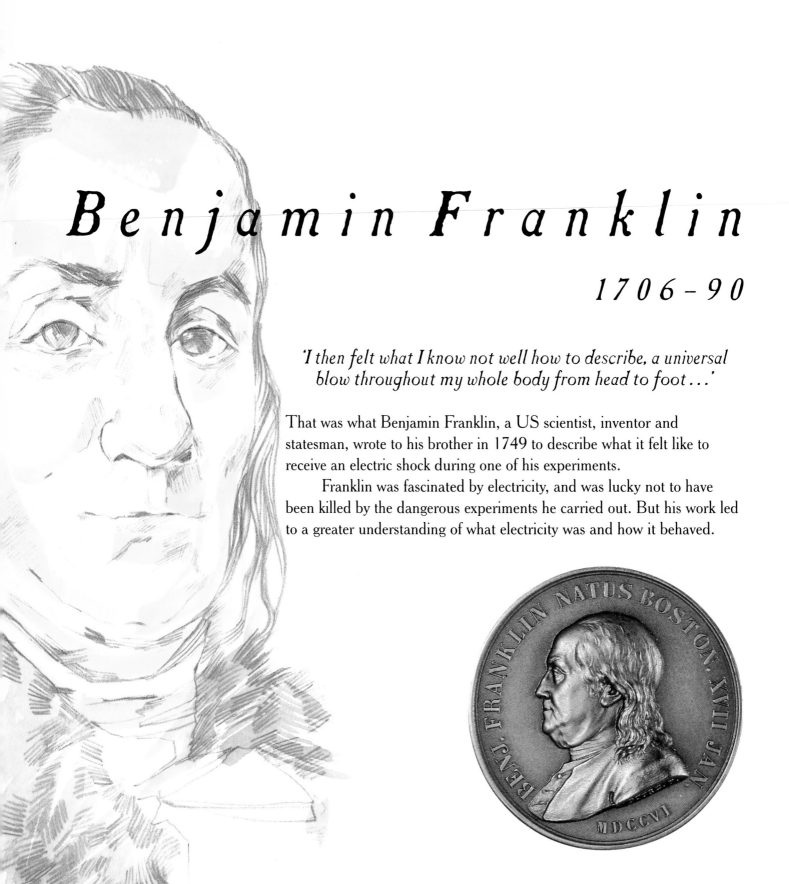

Benjamin Franklin

1706 - 90

'I then felt what I know not well how to describe, a universal blow throughout my whole body from head to foot...'

That was what Benjamin Franklin, a US scientist, inventor and statesman, wrote to his brother in 1749 to describe what it felt like to receive an electric shock during one of his experiments.

Franklin was fascinated by electricity, and was lucky not to have been killed by the dangerous experiments he carried out. But his work led to a greater understanding of what electricity was and how it behaved.

A portrait of Benjamin Franklin, on a medal.

Benjamin Franklin was born in 1706 in Boston, Massachusetts, USA. When he was just 10 years old he began working with his father as a soap and candle maker. When he was 12 he was apprenticed to his brother as a printer. By the time he was 24 he had set up his own printing business in Philadelphia. There, Franklin published a newspaper and began printing *Poor Richard's Almanack* – a yearly book full of facts, figures and wise sayings which he wrote himself, such as:

'Early to bed and early to rise, makes a man healthy, wealthy and wise.'

This page from *Poor Richard's Almanack* shows symbols of the Zodiac and illustrations of the activities which take place in March, July, September, November and December.

In his spare time, Franklin began to study science. In 1743, he helped to found the American Philosophical Society. Like the Royal Society in Britain, the Philosophical Society aimed to encourage interest and research in science.

Franklin's printing business was so successful that he was able to retire when he was 42 and spend more time conducting scientific experiments. He invented many practical things, including an efficient stove, known as the Franklin stove. He also looked into many scientific subjects, including oceanography (the study of the sea), the weather and light. But his greatest interest was in electricity.

OTHERS TO STUDY

Abbé Jean Antoine Nollet (1700–70) – a French priest who was famous for his research on electricity.

Joseph Priestly (1733–1804) – a British chemist who conducted experiments in electricity and published a book called *The History of Electricity* in 1767. He was also the first person to isolate oxygen.

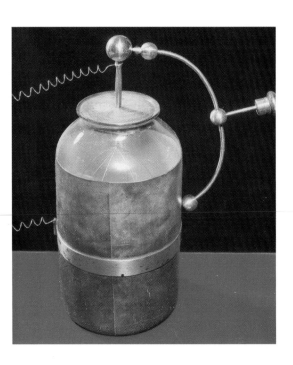

A Leyden jar. These glass jars, which were coated inside and out with metal, were used to store static electricity. They were used by many scientists interested in learning about electricity.

In his electrical experiments, Franklin often used a Leyden jar. This was a glass jar coated both inside and out with metal, which could be used to store **static electricity**.

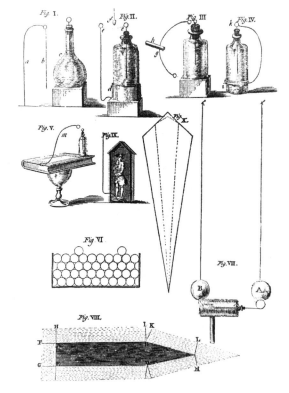

Some of the drawings Franklin made to illustrate his experiments. The drawings at the top show how Franklin made use of a Leyden jar in his work.

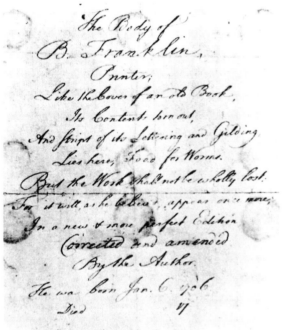

Franklin discovered that lightning was a form of electricity when he flew a kite fitted with a pointed wire during a thunderstorm. In this drawing, his idea is being tested by allowing lightning to strike a long metal pole. When the lightning touched the upper part of the pole, a spark could be drawn off near its base.

Later, Franklin became interested in finding out more about the nature of lightning in the sky. In 1752 he flew a kite fitted with a pointed wire during a thunderstorm. In one hand he held a silk thread attached to the kite. When lightning flashed, he put his other hand near a metal key lying on the ground and observed a spark leaping across the gap. This showed that lightning was a form of electricity, and led to the invention of the **lightning rod**. Although Franklin was not hurt during the experiment, it was a very dangerous one. The next two people who tried it were both killed.

As well as being a scientist, Franklin was also a politician. He helped to write the ***American Declaration of Independence***, and travelled to Europe to explain the American point of view during the War of Independence, when the US went to war with Britain to fight for a free country. After the war was over, he helped to negotiate peace. When he died in 1790, Franklin was known throughout the world as a politician, ingenious inventor and scientist whose work has inspired many other scientists ever since.

Before he died, Franklin wrote this amusing verse to go on his own tombstone:
The Body of
B. Franklin
Printer;
Like the leaves of an old book
Its Contents torn out,
And stript of its lettering and Guilding
Lies here, Food for Worms.
But the Work shall not be wholly lost:
For it will, as he believes, appear once more;
In a new and more perfect Edition
Corrected and amended
By the Author.

He was born Jan. 6 1706
Died 17..

Antoine Lavoisier

1743 - 94

'[He] discovered no new body, no new property, no natural **phenomenon** *previously unknown. His immortal glory consists in this – he infused into the body of science a new spirit.'*

This is how a nineteenth-century German chemist, Justus von Liebig, described the French scientist Antoine Lavoisier.

Lavoisier's ideas changed the face of chemistry. His great achievement was putting chemistry into a form of language which is still understood by chemists today.

Antoine Lavoisier with his wife Marie-Anne, who helped him with all his scientific work.

Antoine Lavoisier was born in Paris on 26 August 1743, the son of a wealthy lawyer. Although he graduated with a degree in law from the Collège des Quatre Nations, and later joined an organization which collected taxes for the French government, his real interest was in science.

As a young man, Lavoisier helped a friend to map the **geology** of France. But soon his imagination turned to chemistry, and he published his first chemical paper when he was only 22 years old.

Fig.1

Antoine Lavoisier carrying out experiments to prove that it is air, rather than the mysterious substance phlogiston, which is important in burning. During these experiments, Lavoisier carefully burned different materials and measured how their weight changed.

In the mid-eighteenth century, chemistry was very difficult to understand, because each substance was often known by several different names. Lavoisier worked with four other French chemists to develop a new system of naming chemicals. This system organized chemical information to make it easy to use. Lavoisier used the new system in his book, *Traité Élémentaire de Chimie* (Elements of Chemistry), which was published in 1789.

DATE CHART

1743
26 August: Antoine Lavoisier is born in Paris.

1764
Begins working on chemistry and publishes his first chemical paper.

1768
Is elected to the French Academy of Sciences, and joins the tax-collecting organization.

1787
Publishes *Méthode de Nomenclature Chimique (Method of Chemical Nomenclature)* with two other French chemists.

1789
Traité Élémentaire de Chimie is published.

1794
8 May: Lavoisier is executed during the French Revolution.

Lavoisier's book was the first 'modern' chemistry book. Although chemists today find it very hard to understand the language in earlier chemistry books, they find Lavoisier's writings fairly easy to read.

Lavoisier also proved that the phlogiston theory was wrong. This theory was put forward in 1718 by a Bavarian professor of medicine, Georg Stahl. It said that some materials contained a mysterious substance called phlogiston, which was released when the material was burnt. Belief in this theory had held back progress in chemistry for many years.

By carefully burning different materials and observing how their weight changed, Lavoisier showed that it was air, rather than phlogiston, which was important in burning. This suggested that phlogiston was not a real substance. He also proved that oxygen from the air was absorbed by metals when they were burnt.

In all his laboratory work, Lavoisier was helped by his wife Marie-Anne. She also accompanied her husband when he met with other scientists, and wrote about the meetings. Although Lavoisier never learned English, Marie-Anne did, and she translated English books and papers into French for her husband to read. She also took lessons from the famous artist Jacques Louis David so that she could make engravings to illustrate her husband's papers and books. Along with her husband, she held meetings each week with other scientists to discuss their work.

Lavoisier carrying out experiments to find out which gases are important in breathing. This drawing is based on one made by Lavoisier's wife Marie-Anne. She helped her husband in his work, and is shown sitting at a writing table on the right.

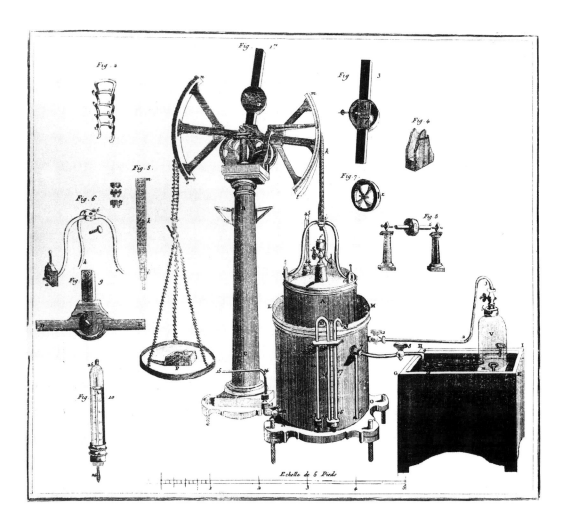

In 1794, during the **French Revolution**, Lavoisier was arrested because of his connection with the tax-collecting organization, and sentenced to death. He was beheaded on 8 May 1794. In his last letter from prison, Lavoisier wrote:

> *'I shall be remembered with some regrets and perhaps leave some reputation behind me. What more can I ask?'*

Lavoisier was right about being remembered. He was greatly missed by many scientists of his time:

> *'Only a moment to cut off that head and a hundred years may not give us another like it.'*

This was written by a fellow French scientist, Joseph Louis Lagrange, with great sadness. No chemist working today can ever forget the work Lavoisier did to bring chemistry into the modern age.

OTHERS TO STUDY

Claude-Louis Berthollet (1748–1822)
– a French chemist who worked with Lavoisier and helped him to write *Méthode de Nomenclature Chimique*.

Antoine François Fourcroy (1755–1809)
– a French teacher and modernizer of chemistry who promoted Lavoisier's theories.

Joseph Louis Lagrange (1736–1813)
– a French mathematician who admired Lavoisier's work.

Alessandro Volta

1745-1827

One day in 1786, Luigi Galvani, a professor of anatomy at the University of Bologna, Italy, was sitting near a machine which gave off electric sparks and cutting up a dead frog in order to study it. Suddenly, to his surprise, the frog's leg twitched. He found that the frog's leg twitched even more during stormy weather, especially if he used a brass hook to hang it from an iron railing. Galvani wondered why this happened, and began to carry out experiments to find out more.

Galvani believed his experiments proved the existence of animal electricity – a theory which claimed that animal nerves and muscles contained an electric fluid. But Galvani was wrong.

Luigi Galvani experimenting with 'animal electricity'. Galvani found that if he touched a frog's leg hung from a brass hook on an iron stand with a metal wire, it twitched.

OTHERS TO STUDY

Joseph Banks (1743–1820) – a British botanist who was president of the Royal Society for 42 years. He took an interest in Volta's work.

Humphrey Davy (1778–1829) – a British scientist who made use of Volta's battery to discover the elements sodium and potassium.

Michael Faraday (1791–1867) – an assistant to Davy who invented the dynamo. He carried out research into electricity which made Volta's battery possible.

When the Italian physicist Alessandro Volta read about Galvani's work in 1791, he realized that the frog's leg twitched because of the difference in **electrical potential** between the copper in the brass hook and the iron in the railings. The frog's leg connected the two metals and allowed an electric current to pass through.

Volta went on to test the electrical potential between other pairs of metals, and found that different pairs had different electrical potentials. He used this information to build a working battery. This was the first time anyone had produced a source of continuous electrical current.

Volta described his 'striking results' in a letter written in 1800 to Joseph Banks, President of the Royal Society:

'... the apparatus of which I speak, and which will, without doubt, astonish you, is no more than a collection of different types of good conductors arranged in a particular manner.'

Volta's battery consisted of 'cells' made of two different metals, usually silver and zinc, which were separated by disks of cardboard soaked in water. The cells were called galvanic cells, after Luigi Galvani. The battery gave off an electric current when the cells were connected. The electrical potential was measured in volts, named after Alessandro Volta himself.

Volta's battery opened up many new possibilities for studying electricity, and led to the discovery of two new metal elements, sodium and potassium.

Alessandro Volta.

A galvanometer. This instrument, for detecting and measuring small electric currents, is named after Galvani, and was used by Volta in his experiments on electricity.

Glossary

Abstain To refuse to do something.

American Declaration of Independence A document written in 1776, in which the 13 colonies of the USA declared their independence from Britain.

Astronomy The study of the planets and the stars.

Atom The smallest possible unit of a substance.

Barometer A device for measuring air pressure.

Calculus A type of mathematics.

Cell The basic unit that makes up animals and plants. Some organisms consist of just one cell.

Chemical elements Substances which cannot be split up into separate substances.

Chronometer An instrument that measures time.

Circumference The distance around a circle.

Comet A small body that travels around the Sun in an orbit that is not circular.

Condemned Strongly disapproved of.

Deduce To come up with the answer to a question by studying the known facts.

Elasticity The property some materials have which allows them to be squashed or stretched.

Electrical potential The electrical energy stored in an object.

Fertilize To join together an egg cell and a sperm cell so that a new organism can begin to develop.

Focus To make clearer.

Fossils The remains of plants and animals which are preserved in rocks.

French Revolution A civil war in France, which began in 1789 and ended in 1799. The people of France overthrew their king.

Geology The study of rocks.

House arrest When someone is arrested but is held at home instead of in jail.

Lens A piece of glass with curved surfaces, which makes things look bigger or smaller.

Lightning rod A pointed metal rod or wire, fixed to the outside of a building to carry the electrical charge from lighting safely to the ground.

Lutheran Church A branch of the Protestant Church, founded in 1530 by Martin Luther.

Magnify To enlarge something.

Mechanics A branch of physics which describes how things work.

Natural scientists Scientists who are interested in understanding the workings of nature.

Phenomenon Something new or unusual.

Philosophy The science of thinking and solving problems.

Pressure A force pressing against an object.

Reproduce To produce offspring.

Solicitations Recommendations and good words.

Static electricity Electrical charges which hold on to the surface of an object, but are not able to move through the object. Static electricity is what gives you a shock when you touch a metal object after walking across a nylon carpet.

Theories Ideas about how something works or what something means.

Universal joint A type of joint that can be moved in any direction.

Books to read

Brenda Clarke, *Women and Science* (Wayland, 1989)

John Farman, *A Suspiciously Simple History of Science and Invention without the Boring Bits* (Pan, 1994)

Peter Lafferty, *Pioneers of Science: Leonardo da Vinci* (Wayland, 1990)

Douglas McTavish, *Pioneers of Science: Isaac Newton/Galileo* (Wayland, 1990)

Anne Mountfield, *Women and Education* (Wayland, 1990)

Chris Oxley and Corinne Stockly, *The World of the Microscope* (Usborne, 1989)

Struan Reid and Patricia Farar, *The Usborne Book of Scientists from Archimedes to Einstein* (Usborne, 1992)

Royston Roberts, *Serendipity: Accidental Discoveries in Science* (Wiley, 1989)

Kathryn Senior, *Timelines: Medicine, Doctors, Demons and Drugs* (Watts, 1993)

Tony Triggs, *Tudors and Stuarts: Scientists and Writers* (Wayland, 1993)

Places to visit

The Museum of the History of Science, Oxford. Tel: (01865) 277239
Whipple Museum of the History of Science, Cambridge. Tel: (01223) 334540
Old Royal Observatory, Greenwich, London. Tel: (0181) 858 4422

Science Museum, London. Tel: (0171) 938 8000
Natural History Museum, London. Tel: (0171) 938 9123
Royal Observatory, Edinburgh. Tel: (0131) 668 8100
University Museum, Oxford. Tel: (01865) 270949

_I   n   d   e   x_